90+ herbal teas to be in good health

Nature Passion

A little guide that will not only help you learn about the benefits of certain plants, but also enable you to treat yourself naturally and enjoy these special herbal drinks.

Cristina & Olivier Rebière

TABLE OF CONTENTS

We welcome you in your **Nature Passion: "90+ herbal teas to be in good health"**, a practical guide that we hope will help you to better know the medicinal properties of plants. This may inspire you to start making herbal teas, infusions, and other herbal drinks to improve your health and well-being. Some of these drinks also have exquisite tastes, so we encourage you to try the "potions" presented in this book!

I have always been passionate about plants and often used their properties to treat myself, my little family, and even my friends. I have not hesitated to treat my child's pains such as stomach discomfort, a small wound, a skin irritation, etc. And this has never been a problem. In fact, there have been times when my child could not tolerate conventional medicines, but had no issues with using plant remedies. I am referring to minor pains, but it is important to keep in mind that you should still consult a medical doctor if the problem persists or appears to be more serious! Every child falls and gets scratched - it does not necessarily mean that you must see a doctor. However, it is important to take care of small wounds, as they can easily become infected. The classic disinfectant bought in pharmacy is very useful, but this does not help healing it. Plants do. Same thing for the cold stroke, the cough which does not always calm down with the prescribed syrups, etc.

My curiosity in this area has never stopped since I prefer to treat myself with a good herbal tea rather than taking pills. Several friends have told me that I should write a little book about it, so here I am!

In this book, I will first introduce the properties of some of the most common plants. I will also explain how to prepare them in order to make some herbal teas.

Afterward I will propose you two or three herbal teas by ailment. I am not going to make an exhaustive list of ailments, but those which affect most of the people. The small or large everyday life's pains that can be treated or "calmed" with herbal teas instead of going to buy drugs.

I will present, at the end of this book, a section with ***Herbal drinks for your pleasure*** that will make you discover some drinks that you can prepare and that will also delight your taste buds or refresh yourself.

I imagine that, like me, you do not have an infallible memory. This small guide will help you remember quickly and easily which plants and herbal teas can help you if you have problems of blood circulation, cholesterol, kidney stones, if you have a fleeting anemia or if you have just a low energy...

Be careful, herbal teas are not going to cure you and will definitely not take the place of doctor's recommendations. However, plants are an invaluable source of vitamins, minerals and other nutrients. They have been used for millennia for their properties. Several hundred medicinal plants are known and their use is systematized by the phytotherapy.

I will not pretend to present you all the plants that exist because I would have to write a whole encyclopedia! However, I have already written other small guides in this collection ***Nature Passion***.

I have always preferred drinking a herbal tea to treat myself rather than a pill, and it has been working. For years :-)... So why not switch to the "natural" way of things... or, better said, come back to it ?!?

Furthermore, plants were the primary inspiration behind my children's book series: **"Cathy Merlin"**. I wanted to make children aware of the benefits of plants, to teach them some properties that can really serve them later... How many times I have not treated myself or the others with this incredible plant "*Plantago major*" or greater plantain (that you are going to find within the next section) that can be found almost everywhere and is almost regarded as a weed? This plant has always impressed me: so banal and common, but with such exceptional properties! Considered often as a bad grass or weed, I learned some of its properties as a child.

I remember that one day I had a paronychia to one of my hand's fingers. Pus was accumulating under my skin and I was threatened with an operation that I did not want! So I tried what the doctor suggested me: compresses with solutions purchased at the pharmacy. Yet, my finger did not seem to deflate at all and became more and more ugly... You can see some photos on Wikipedia to understand what I'm talking about if you never had seen or had such a paronychia... But an old granny told me about this "greater plantain" and even showed it to me because it's such a common herb that is found everywhere in the temperate zones. Really everywhere!

As far as the operation frightened me, I tried the advice of that granny: I took two leaves and washed them, then put them around my finger by making a bandage tight enough. A few minutes later my finger began to pulsate. Stronger and stronger... For ten minutes it pulsed so hard that it certainly could not be my imagination! I also kept in mind that I had to change the leaf, putting a fresh one every two-three hours since, according to what the granny had told me, the leaf "pulled" the pus out and then lost its qualities. So I waited two hours. My finger had stopped pulsing for some time. By opening the very rough bandage (since it has only the role to hold the leaf tightly on the spot) I noticed with surprise that my finger had decreased in volume... and it looked much better! I repeated the operation twice during the day and the next morning when I opened my bandage I had the great joy of discovering that there was no more pus under the skin! Amazing! The finger was still a little red, but I had almost no more pain! Since then I have used and advised the use of greater plantain several times and it has always had the same spectacular results. It is perhaps for this reason that I almost dedicated to this surprising plant my **"Cathy Merlin"** series which was born from my passion for the plants' healing properties :-). If you have children and you want to make them discover a universe of magic, but based on real facts (because full of stories of these books really happened and most of the "magical" properties of plants are true), then go to any online platform and you will surely find them or on our website here http://olivierrebiere.com/livres-numeriques/

What is in fact a herbal tea?

A herbal tea is a beverage with curative properties obtained from fresh or dried plants (flowers, leaves, roots) by **maceration** , **decoction** or **infusion** in hot or cold water.

How to prepare a herbal tea?

There are several ways to prepare a herbal tea:
- by infusion that consists of pouring hot water on the plants and then letting them infuse for a few minutes;
- by **decoction** that consists in bringing to boiling for a few minutes the plants plunged in the water;
- by **maceration** that consists in soaking the plants in cold water for several hours.

Plants can be used fresh or dry.

Which parts of the plant are used to make herbal teas?

The plant is rarely used as a whole and what you should know is that different parts of the same plant can have different uses. The used parts of a plant are generally:
- **root**: rhizome (ginger), bulb (garlic) or root (Angelica),
- **leaves** (laurel, sage, basil),
- **flowers** (marigold, violet)
- **petals** (poppy),
- **aerial parts** (nettle),
- **stem** (horsetail),
- **fruits** (hawthorn)
- **seeds** (flax),
- **bark** (cinnamon),

❀ **buds** (pine).

How to use a herbal tea ?

Infusions and decoctions are preferably consumed hot. However, you can drink them cold as well during the summer and so enjoy refreshing yourself at the same time. When you will start to taste different preparations, some herbal teas will really please you and surprise you with their delicate and fragrant flavor like the one made with cornflowers for example. I am not going to write about plants that are really too bitter or unpleasant because it should also be a pleasure to drink your tea, not only good for your health.

MY ADVICE: It is better not to sweeten your teas since sugar lowers the virtues of plants. However, for plants that have a bitter or too acid taste, honey can successfully replace sugar.

Herbal teas are known for their compositions rich in vitamins, in particular B1 and B2, minerals, and trace elements. If you consume them regularly, you can avoid many deficiencies.

Let's remember the vitamins' role:

- ❀ vitamin A: promotes growth, improves vision, promotes hydration of the skin
- ❀ vitamin B complex: includes several vitamins which mainly play a role in the metabolism of carbohydrates, lipids and proteins, but also in the synthesis of certain hormones
- ❀ vitamin C: needed in the synthesis of collagen and red blood cells, stimulates natural defenses and immunity, antioxidant and anti-scorbutic

- ❀ vitamin D: necessary in early childhood to avoid rickets, reduces the risk of osteoporosis
- ❀ vitamin E: antioxidant, has a protective effect on the red blood cells and a beneficial effect on the cholesterol level
- ❀ vitamin K: helps in the fixation of calcium by bones and has an anti-hemorrhagic effect

You should know that you can use herbal teas for drinking: in this case we speak of internal use. But you can use them also in compresses or for baths of the affected body part (cuts, burns, inflammations, etc.) and then we speak of external use.

In summary, **herbal teas are not only excellent for your health, but they can have a curative effect**. Moreover, they will bring you the nutrients your body needs. Herbal teas can fill or prevent deficiencies and have beneficial effects in various conditions that I am going to present, to facilitate your research.

I will begin by introducing you to the therapeutic virtues of some plants, in alphabetical order, in the next section . I will also tell you which parts of the plant are used, in what form (dry or fresh) and for what types of conditions you can use them.

MY ADVICE: If you cannot find some plants nearby, I advise you to buy them online. There are several websites that deliver this kind of herbal teas. I recommend you to buy dried plants without preservatives in order to be able to extract a maximum of virtues.

Basil - *Ocimum basilicum*

Description, components, used parts

Basil is grown as an aromatic and condimental plant, but its therapeutic virtues are less well known. The leaves are pale to dark green, sometimes purple violet in some varieties. The flowers are small and white and the fine, oblong, black seeds. Basil is known and used since antiquity, when it was considered a royal plant. In the Middle Ages, it was part of the plants of witchcraft.

Leaves and flowering tops are used for herbal teas that have a pleasant aromatic flavor.

Habitat

Currently, basil is very widespread on the planet and used in all the cuisines of the world. You can plant it in your garden and even grow it potted, but be careful because it fears the cold. It enjoys a warm and sunny, Mediterranean or tropical climate.

Tip : You can prevent the appearance of flowers in order to increase leaf production, by pinching the ends of the stems as the flowers form.

Caution: basil herbal teas are not suitable for pregnant or lactating women or for children!

Medicinal properties: Basil has digestive,

antispasmodic, antiseptic, diuretic and anti-inflammatory properties.

Blackcurrant - *Ribes nigrum*

Description, components, used parts

Blackcurrant is the fruit of the *Ribes nigrum* shrub, of black color forming clusters, pulpy, smooth skin, highly aromatic. You all know the excellent blackcurrant jam or the sour juice which is equally delicious, with a beautiful blue flower and lanceolate leaves. Flowering occurs between May and August. The fruits are rich in vitamin C and B, but also in calcium, iron, magnesium, phosphorus and potassium. Fruits and leaves are used for herbal tea.

Habitat

Blackcurrant grows spontaneously in mountainous and cold regions, but is grown in hilly and mountainous areas.

Medicinal properties: Blackcurrant is an excellent fortifier, with healing, anti-fatigue, anti-diarrheal and anti-infectious properties. It has diuretic and depurative properties, stimulates liver and kidney functions. It is beneficial in the treatment of circulatory disorders and hypertension, but also strengthens bones and calms migraines.

Borage - *Borago officinalis*

Description, components, used parts

Borage is a herbaceous plant, with thick and hairy stem. Moreover, the whole plant is covered with short and firm hairs that make it tough to the touch. Flowers are blue.

Leaves are rich in mucilage and potassium nitrate and the seeds are rich in essential fatty acids, including omega-6.

In the Middle Ages, borage was considered an aphrodisiac magic plant.

Habitat

Borage is fairly common in wastelands of temperate zones.

Caution: do not use it excessively and for a too long time.

Medicinal properties: By its mucilage, the borage has emollient and expectorant properties, thus used in inflammations of the respiratory tract and gastritis. It is also diuretic and depurative.

Breckland thyme - *Thymus serpyllum*

Description, components, used parts

This thyme (*Thymus serpyllum*) is a sub-shrub about 10 cm in height, extending up to 50 cm in width. It has very small, opposite, oval or lanceolate leaves with a lemon odor and upright blue or purple floral stems.

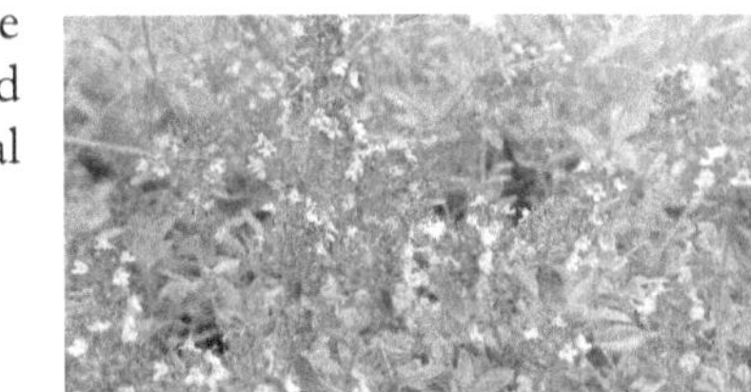

9

The aerial parts are dried for therapeutic purposes.
Habitat
The thyme is a plant of the sunny areas, brush, dry meadows, rockeries, up to 3.000 m altitude.

Medicinal properties: The thyme has antiseptic, anti-viral, diuretic, expectorant and antispasmodic properties. It disinfects the digestive tract. It is used in mouthwash in case of inflammation of the gums and gargle in case of irritation of the throat or angina. It is beneficial for migraines.

Celery - *Apium graveolens*

Description, components, used parts
The celery (*Apium graveolens L.*) is a herbaceous plant, grown for its leaves and its root, eaten as a vegetable. Celery contains vitamin A, B, C and K. Celery is very low in calories and rich in antioxidants.

Caution: celery leaves contain phototoxic furanocoumarins which can cause skin accidents in case of exposure to the sun after prolonged contact with the plant or excessive ingestion.

Medicinal properties: Celery purifies the blood, helps in increasing the number of red blood cells. It is useful for fighting against constipation, migraines, and rheumatism. Celery has diuretic and tonic properties. It is also beneficial in case of arterial hypertension, in bronchial ailments and it fights stress, with a relaxing action on the nervous system.

Cherry

Description, components, used parts
Cherry is the fruit that you obviously know, but do you

know the amazing properties of cherry tails?

Fruits also have virtues, but the dried cherries tails are used for herbal tea and have a fruit-like flavor.

Medicinal properties: The tails of dried cherries help the functioning of the kidneys, have a beneficial effect in the urinary ailments and the gout.

Chicory - *Cichorium intybus*

Description, components, used parts

Wild or bitter chicory (*Cichorium intybus* L.) is a herbaceous plant with blue flowers, oval, elongated, sharp-pointed toothed leaves. All parts of the plant are bitter ; leaves and roots are used for herbal tea. It is rich in inulin (especially in the root), but also contains vitamin B, C, and K.

Habitat

Wild chicory is very common in meadows, uncultivated fields and roadside in Europe, Asia and North Africa.

Medicinal properties: Chicory stimulates drainage and is beneficial to the liver and kidneys. It improves intestinal transit.

Cornflower - *Centaurea cyanus*

Description, components, used parts

The cornflower is a herbaceous plant, with a beautiful blue flower and lanceolate leaves. Flowering occurs between May and August. The flowers are rich in magnesium.

Habitat

Cornflowers are often present in the vicinity of cereal fields and in flowery fields.

Medicinal properties: Cornflower has anti-rheumatic, febrifuge and diuretic properties. It calms irritations and inflammations of the skin and the eyes.

Couch grass - *Elymus repens*

Description, components, used parts

Quackgrass or couch grass is a herbaceous plant, very lively because of its rhizomes and considered most often as a weed invading crops and gardens. It can grow up to 1 m tall, has erected, flattened flowers and flattened, acute leaves. The rhizomes are very branched, long, white. The rhizome is used in herbal teas. It contains potassium, iron and vitamin B.

Medicinal properties: The rhizomes of couch grass have emollient, antibacterial, antifungal and diuretic properties. Herbal teas are beneficial for hypertension, respiratory, urinary and joint diseases.

Cowberry - Vaccinum vitis idaea

Description, components, used parts

Cowberry is a sub-shrub, 10 to 30 cm tall, with evergreen

leaves, 15 to 40 mm long, rounded, with coiled edges, green shining above and light green below. Its flowers appear from May to August and are bell-shaped, white or rosy, grouped in clusters. Its fruits, 5 to 10 mm in diameter, are red and have an acidulous flavor. Fruits are mostly harvested in September and October. Cowberry fruits contain a lot of vitamin C. They are rich in minerals and antioxidants.

Habitat

Cowberry Is found in the Arctic, northern Eurasia, Japan and North America. In France, it is quite encountered in the Jura area and the Alps up to 3 000 m altitude. The Cowberry grows in light woods (pine, spruce, beech and fir), peat bogs and mountain lawns.

Medicinal properties: Cowberry is a plant with a predominantly female orientation. It is recommended in menopause, but also for urogenital inflammations such as cystitis. It also has anti-inflammatory, antiseptic, astringent and diuretic properties.

Dandelion - *Taraxacum officinalis*

Description, components, used parts

Dandelion is a perennial plant that everyone knows, recognizable by its yellow flowers. It has a long root, fusiform, the size of a finger, brown-reddish. The leaves, arranged in rosette at the base of the plant, are green and divided with acute and toothed lobes.

Leaves and roots are dried for therapeutic purposes.

Habitat

Dandelion grows everywhere in fields, meadows, light woods, along roadsides or rivers.

Medicinal properties: Dandelions have diuretic, depurative, detoxifying, mineralizing, calming and sedative properties. This plant is beneficial for liver problems.

<u>Dog-rose - *Rosa canina*</u>

Description, components, used parts
The dog-rose is a species of thorny shrubs of the rosaceae family, very common in temperate regions. It can reach 3 m high and its leaves are alternate and toothed. The flowers called rose hips have a simple corolla with five petals of white-rosy color. The fruits are red when they are ripe (October) and are called "cynorrhodons" and are very rich in sugars and vitamin C, but also in vitamin B and A. They are in fact  derived from the transformation of the floral receptacle (false fruit), which contains the real fruits (= achenes).

Caution: the fruits (achenes) and the hairs contained inside the rose hip have a very irritating effect on the skin and the mucosa. Their contact causes severe itching and their ingestion causes a very important anal pruritus (that's why its popular name is ass-scraper).

The fruits can be harvested from July to October, dried and used for therapeutic purposes.

Habitat
Dog-rose is common in Europe in hedges, underbrush and uncultivated land, in the woods especially in the plain.

Medicinal properties: The fruits are beneficial against fatigue, colds, diarrhea. It is an excellent venous tonic which also has mineralizing properties, diuretics.

<u>Elderberry - *Sambucus nigra*</u>

Description, components, used parts
The Great Elder or Black Elder is a species of fast-growing shrubs of 1 to 10 meters in height. Its leaves are

regularly serrated and have an unpleasant odor when crushed. The flowers appear in early summer and are creamy white with a fairly pronounced pleasant scent. The fruits are small purplish black berries of 6-8 mm soft flesh arranged in clusters, with three seeds.

Elderberry fruits contain vitamin A and C.

Flowers and fruits are dried for therapeutic purposes. With the fresh flowers an excellent refreshing drink can be made. You will find the recipe in the section Herbal drinks for your pleasure.

Habitat

The elderberry is found in Europe, West Asia and North Africa in the plain and on the hills.

Medicinal properties: Elderflowers have a sudorific, diuretic, emollient action. They are beneficial for rheumatism and stimulate the immunity of the body. Fruits have laxative and anti-neuralgic properties.

Euphrasia rostkoviana - *Euphrasia officinalis*

Description, components, used parts

Euphrasia rostkoviana is a herbaceous plant with oval toothed leaves, with pretty little white flowers, yellow throat and lilac upper lip. It is also called eyeglass breakers or myopic grass, thanks to its ophthalmic properties. The whole plant is used dried to make herbal teas.

Medicinal properties: Euphrasia rostkoviana has anti-inflammatory, anti-allergic and anti-infectious properties. It is beneficial for conjunctivitis and hay fever.

<h1 style="text-align:center">Ail - Allium sativum</h1>

Description, components, used parts

You know all the garlic and you use it in your kitchen ... I will not describe it to you. You have also surely heard that it has medicinal properties, but do you really know all its virtues?

Garlic contains vitamin A, B1, B2 and C, but also allicin, an anti-bacterial, anti-infectious compound that combats viruses. The used parts are the bulb (the garlic cloves you use most commonly in the kitchen), but also the young leaves. Both are consumed raw to take advantage of their medicinal properties.

Habitat

You can plant it easily in your garden and even potted on your terrace or buy it directly at the market.

Medicinal properties: Garlic is a very beneficial plant that is used to fight against colds and bronchitis. It has anti-bacterial effects and helps to fight against skin disorders such as acne and blackheads. Garlic has a diuretic action, facilitates digestion and has anti-infectious properties. It lowers blood pressure and increases the fluidity of the blood. Garlic has very good disinfectant and bactericidal qualities and can therefore help to treat mycoses and warts (by reducing the garlic mashed and applying it to the area concerned). To keep it in place put on a compress and stick with plaster).

<h1 style="text-align:center">Ginger - Zingiber officinalis</h1>

Description, components, used parts

Ginger (Zingiber officinale) is a plant whose rhizome has been used in traditional medicine since Antiquity.

Ginger is rich in potassium, zinc, calcium, copper and magnesium, and vitamin B, C and D. The fresh or dried rhizome is used for herbal teas.

Medicinal properties:

Ginger lowers cholesterol levels, is effective against nausea and transport ailments. It has an anti-inflammatory action, being beneficial for inflammatory rheumatism.

Greater plantain - *Plantago major*

Description, components, used parts

The greater plantain is a plant that has always fascinated me. It is considered today more like a weed by the farmers, but it was nevertheless one of the first to have been spread in the colonies ... Would it not thanks to its virtues???

You will quickly recognize it in parks, lawns or on the paths of the woods with its green leaves, oval and broad that are arranged in rosette. Its inflorescence has many tiny flowers.

Habitat

The greater plantain is found everywhere in temperate zones. It is an ancient medicinal plant whose leaves and seeds are used. Since antiquity, this plant is considered to be haemostatic with rapid action on wounds - ie it has the ability to stop hemorrhages.

Medicinal properties: The greater plantain has depurative, diuretic, antimicrobial, antiallergic, anti-inflammatory, healing and haemostatic properties. It is beneficial in respiratory ailments and especially the syrup based on this plant is excellent for the cough since it fluidifies the secretions of the bronchi. The seeds are laxative by mechanical effect due to the mucilage they contain. This plant also helps to lower cholesterol and hypertension and purifies the blood and lungs.

Hawthorn - *Crataegus monogyna*

Description, components, used parts
The hawthorn is a shrub that can measure from 4 to 10 m with spiny and smooth branches. The flowers are white or pink, very fragrant, in bouquets. The fruits are red, oval form, with a single nucleus. Fruits and flowers are used in infusions. The flowers and fruits of the hawthorn contain vitamin B and C.

Habitat
The hawthorn is very common all over France up to 1,600 m altitude. It is frequently found in the hedgerows of temperate zones of Western Europe.

Medicinal properties: The flowers of the hawthorn have qualities of regulating the heart rhythm and improving the coronary circulation. It is a hypotensive, cardiotonic and an antispasmodic, which calms the palpitations. The hawthorn in herbal tea reduces the stress and facilitates the sleep, but in high doses can have a contrary effect!

MY ADVICE: If you want to pick hawthorn flowers, be aware that the flowering period is short. It is necessary to pick the flowers when they are in bud, otherwise the petals would come off on drying. Have them dry in a ventilated place. The flowers must barely yellow and keep their odor. Once dried, store them in a cardboard box or paper bags.

Horsetail - *Equisetum arvense*

Description, components, used parts

Horsetail is a perennial rhizome plant with two types of stems: some, sterile, ranging from 50 cm to 1 m, robust, erect, striated, hollow and the other fertile, smaller, appear before the previous ones at the beginning of spring, reddish-brown, thicker with an oblong spike. Horsetail is very rich in silica, but also in potassium, calcium, iron and vitamin C. Green stems are dried for therapeutic purposes.

Habitat

Common in Europe, the horsetail is widespread in the wetlands of temperate zones and can rise up to 2,500 m altitude.

Medicinal properties: Horsetail has a mineralizing, antiseptic, anti-inflammatory and diuretic effect. It is beneficial for osteoporosis, atherosclerosis, arthritis, kidney and liver problems. It is a good fortifier of hair and nails.

Hyssop - *Hyssopus officinalis*

Description, components, used parts

The hyssop is a plant with violet, blue, white or red flowers. It is a plant that prefers the sunny locations in a rather dry and well-drained soil. It calms dental pain if the infusion is used for gargling.

Habitat

Hyssop has been cultivated for a very long time, in the

"gardens of simple", monks and other medieval gardens.

It is a very old medicinal plant from which all the aerial parts are used: flowers, stems and leaves.

Caution: do not use it for children!

Medicinal properties: Hyssop has antiseptic, expectorant and stimulating properties. Herbal teas are beneficial for cough, flu, respiratory ailments such as asthma.

Lamb's-ear - *Stachys byzantina*

Description, components, used parts
Lamb's-ear is a plant called like this because of the slender form and the duvet of its gray-white leaves. The flower corolla is purplish pink and has a concave upper lip.
Habitat
It can be grown easily, adapted to dry climates and rapid growth. It is a very ancient medicinal plant: the Egyptians smoked its leaves to treat many ailments, including injuries, digestive problems and breathing difficulties.

Medicinal properties: Its leaves were used to help wound healing.

Laurel - *Laurus nobilis*

Description, components, used parts
The laurel is a species of shrubs with evergreen foliage, 2 m tall and that can reach up to fifteen meters of height. Leaves, of lanceolate form, have a strong aromatic odor when crushed. The flowers are small, whitish, grouped in umbels. Dried leaves are used in herbal teas.

Habitat
It is a Mediterranean shrub.

Medicinal properties: Its leaves are used to treat abdominal cramps, calm rheumatism, joint pain and dental infections. They have antiseptic, antifungal and stimulating properties.

Lavender - *Lavandula angustifolia*

Description, components, used parts
Lavender is a species of sub-shrub. It is composed of floral stems with an ear with blue-violet flowers. The stem is woody gray-green in color, as its leaves that have an elongated and pointed shape. The plant has a very pronounced specific perfume.

The dried flowers are used in herbal teas.

Habitat
It is a plant originating from the mountainous and sunny areas of the Mediterranean, but it is grown in Europe, Australia and the United States for its properties.

Medicinal properties: Its flowers have calming, antidepressant and sedative properties. They also have an analgesic, anti-inflammatory, antiseptic, antibacterial, diuretic and healing effect. Lavender has hypotensive and antispasmodic qualities. It is used for therapeutic baths for circulatory problems and to alleviate the pain of rheumatism.

Lemon

Components
The lemon contains a lot of vitamin C, but also vitamin A, B and E. It is rich in calcium, potassium, magnesium, iron and zinc. Lemons are also sources of antioxidants.

Medicinal properties: Lemon is antiviral, antibacterial, recommended in heart disease, liver disease, obesity and hair loss. It is also diuretic.

Lemon balm - *Melissa officinalis*

Description, components, used parts
Lemon balm is a perennial plant 30 to 80 cm tall with oval and serrated leaves that give off a soft, lemon-like fragrance when crushed. The flowers are small, white, bell-shaped.

Fresh or dried leaves and stems are used in herbal teas.
Habitat
Originally from Europe, lemon balm has been introduced in North America and has been cultivated and used since ancient times.

Medicinal properties: Stems and leaves are still used as a tonic and light stimulant. Lemon balm has digestive, antiviral, anti-inflammatory, antiseptic and sedative properties. It is beneficial for nausea, tachycardia, stomach and colon spasms.

Lime tree - *Tilia europea*

Description, components, used parts
The lime tree is a large tree up to about thirty meters high, with branches fairly widely spread. The trunk presents a bark at first gray and smooth, then marked with fine longitudinal cracks quite apart. The leaves are simple, alternate, heart-shaped with a long pointed end and toothed edge. The flowers are grouped, each of these group having at their base a peduncle welded along its length to an oblong and translucent bract, yellowish in color. They are very fragrant. Common lime blossoms contain mucilage, essential oils, tannins, manganese and vitamin C. Flowers are dried for

therapeutic purposes, but also its bark.

Habitat

Very common in the plain and hilly regions of the temperate zones, the lime tree is very present in the cities so that you can pick the flowers often by yourself ;-).

Medicinal properties: Lime herbal teas are recommended for fatigue, anxiety attacks, neurasthenia, migraines, flu and insomnia. These flowers are anti-depressants, euphoria and sedatives. They would also be antispasmodic, and would make the blood more fluid and promote circulation.

Linen (or Flax) - *Linum usitatissimum*

Description, components, used parts

Flax (*Linum usitatissimum*) is a herbaceous plant, native to Eurasia, cultivated for its textile fibers and oilseeds. On its stem, nearly one meter long, there are simple, lanceolate leaves. Its flowers are blue or white. The seeds are small, smooth, flat, oblong and very rich in oil. It is one of the oldest cultivated plants in the world.

Seeds are used for herbal teas. They contain magnesium and potassium, but also vitamin E and F.

Medicinal properties: Flax has an emollient action, protecting the mucous membranes of the digestive tract. It is beneficial in gastritis, enteritis, cough, hemorrhoids and cardiovascular diseases. It has laxative, anti-inflammatory properties. It reduces the risk of infarction.

Lovage - *Levisticum officinale*

Description, components, used parts

The lovage is a perennial herb. Its cut leaves resemble those of celery. The inflorescence is a compound, dense, umbel with small yellowish-colored flowers. The seeds are brown and edible. All parts of the plant are used. In phytotherapy, rhizome and dried roots are used as well as the essential oil extracted from the roots.

Habitat

It grows in the Alps, the Pyrenees and the Caucasus below 1.800 m altitude. It is known and cultivated for its phytotherapeutic virtues for a very long time and used as condiment in many countries.

Medicinal properties: Seeds, leaves and roots effectively combat water retention and facilitate the elimination of toxins. The root has anti-convulsive, sedative, digestive, anti-inflammatory, antibacterial, antifungal, antiparasitic and expectorant virtues. The liver has a regulating action on the menstruation, stimulating for the appetite and the liver and biliary functions. Lovage herbal tea is beneficial for migraine and in slimming cures.

Marigold - *Calendula officinalis*

Description, components, used parts

The marigold is a herbaceous plant with yellow or orange-yellow flowers, blooming from the first days of spring and can last almost the whole year. The flowers have the characteristic to close at night and re-open as soon as the sun is high enough in the sky. The marigold was also called "the rain flower" since when it did not open it was a sign that the weather would degrade.

All parts of the marigold have a strong aromatic odor, unpleasant, and their flavor is quite bitter. Flowers are dried for therapeutic purposes.

Habitat

Very common in the Mediterranean regions, the marigold grows in most

gardens and wastelands without needing to be sown there. It is also cultivated and as a matter of fact that was a culture that we practiced in school when I was young in Romania. When I was in primary school, we were mainly concerned with the harvesting and drying of flowers.

Medicinal properties: The marigold has anti-inflammatory, antimicrobial, antioxidant, antiviral, antiseptic, antifungal and cicatrizing properties. It stimulates immune defenses and is beneficial for ulcers. Marigold creams are effective for dermatitis and protect the skin.

Mint - *Mentha piperita*

Description, components, used parts
Peppermint (*Mentha piperita*) is a herbaceous plant derived from spontaneous hybridization between watermint and spearmint. It is a perennial plant of 10 to 80 cm in height with simple hairy leaves, oval-lanceolate with toothed margin that give off a characteristic scent. The flowers are small, pale violet.

The peoples of Antiquity knew and used several species of mints. Due to the peppery flavor of its leaves, it is sparsely used in the kitchen and reserved for medicinal use. The mint tea has nevertheless a pleasant taste and its rather fast effect on abdominal cramps and digestive problems always astonished me. Fresh or dried leaves are used in herbal teas.

Habitat
Mint is grown in Europe, America, Asia and North Africa. The mint found on the roadside is the spearmint, but it also possesses a large part of the properties of the cultivated species.

Medicinal properties: As for all mints, tradition attributes to peppermint tonic and strengthening properties, but also digestive (combat heaviness, bloating, gas, cramps, diarrhea). Mint facilitates the functions of urinary and digestive elimination.

Motherwort - *Leonurus cardiaca*

Description, components, used parts
Motherwort (*Leonurus cardiaca*) is a perennial plant, present throughout Europe. It can reach 1.20 m and its leaves are dark green on top and ashy beneath. The flowers are purplish pink, tightly over the length of the stem with a fluffy appearance. Leaves and flowers are used.

Motherwort contains vitamin A, C, E, beta-carotene, minerals and organic acids.

Habitat
Motherwort is found along the roadsides or forests, in the clearings, on the land left fallow.

Medicinal properties: Motherwort is used to calm spasms in nervous disorders and palpitations, as well as in the treatment of diarrhea, bronchitis and bloating. The herbal tea that can be used as a sedative is effective in insomnia, but also proves useful in depressive states and also at menopause.

Narrow-leaved purple coneflower - *Echinacea Angustifolia*

Description, components, used parts
Narrow-leaved purple coneflower is a flowering plant

known to the Native Americans of the Rocky Mountains for a long time. It has become one of the most widely used medicinal plants in North America and Europe. Flowering occurs from July to September. It is the root and flowers that are used dried.

Habitat

Native to North America, this Echinacea is found in sparse dry woods, meadows and moors, and cultivated land. It can be grown in temperate regions. The planting is done in the spring or the autumn, in a sunny or half-shaded place.

Caution: do not use for pregnant women and children!

Medicinal properties: Narrow-leaved purple coneflower has immunostimulatory activity and healing and antidepressant properties. Herbal teas are beneficial during colds, but also for urinary infections.

Nettle - *Urtica dioica*

Description, components, used parts

The nettles are a genus of about thirty species of herbaceous plants with hairy leaves, most of which have the unfortunate property of "pricking" or burning the skin when inadvertently touched. They have been recognized as one of the most useful and effective medicinal plants for a long time. The whole plant is covered with stinging hairs, so be careful to wear gloves if you want to pick it ;-). The male and female flowers are separated, either on the same foot or on different ones. The female flowers are greenish and hanging,  while the male flowers are yellowish and horizontal, spread out or spiked.

Nettle is rich in vitamins A, B, C and K, but also iron, calcium, magnesium, potassium and phosphorus.

Young leaves, but also the root are used in herbal teas.

Habitat

Nettle grows in cultivated or non-cultivated fields, forests, along roadsides or rivers.

Medicinal properties: The nettles are used as tonic, depurative, diuretic, anti-inflammatory, analgesic, antimicrobial, anti-ulcer, anti-anemic, hepatoprotective, antioxidant, antiallergic and immunostimulant. They are beneficial for rheumatic pains. In mouthwash, nettle is effective against infections such as canker sores or gingivitis. For pregnant women, it promotes lactation.

Orange

Components

The orange is rich in vitamin C, but also contains vitamin A, B, K and E. It contains a lot of potassium, but also calcium, iron phosphorus, copper and zinc. Orange contains antioxidants.

Medicinal properties: Orange is beneficial for nausea, rheumatism, respiratory and skin conditions, anemia, insomnia and asthma.

Oregano - *Origanum vulgare*

Description, components, used parts

Oregano or wild marjoram is a perennial plant 30-80 cm tall, with a red, hairy stem and round, green, slightly toothed leaves. The flowers are small, pink or purple, and grouped in small panicles. It contains iron, calcium, manganese, vitamin E and K. Leaves, seeds and flowers are used in herbal teas.

Habitat

Originally from Europe, oregano was exported to the Middle East. It was known by the peoples of Antiquity for its pronounced taste and its medicinal properties.

Medicinal properties: Oregano has antiseptic, digestive, antifungal, antiviral and expectorant virtues. It is beneficial for fighting stress, lowering cholesterol, decreasing cardiovascular risk.

Persil

Description, components, used parts

Parsley leaves are very rich in vitamin A and C. Parsley contains calcium, iron, magnesium, phosphorus, sodium, potassium.

Medicinal properties: The root of parsley is diuretic, vermifuge. Its action is beneficial for asthenia, anorexia, hypertension, arthritis and rheumatism.

Poppy - Papaver rhoeas

Description, components, used parts

The poppy is a herbaceous plant that you probably know. The flower is red and the stem is fine and hairy. The dried petals have been used since antiquity to calm the pain.

Habitat

Wild poppies are very common in meadows, cultivated fields, cereal fields and form colonies among weeds.

Medicinal properties: Herbal teas have soothing and sedative effects for adults, but also for children. They calm the cough and irritations of the throat.

Queen of the Meadow - *Filipendula Ulmaria*

Description, components, used parts

The Meadowsweet or queen of the meadow is a perennial plant with small, yellowish-white, very fragrant flowers. The leaves are dark green, glabrous above, but felted white below. Leaves, roots and flowers are dried for therapeutic purposes.

Habitat

It grows in wet places, especially along the edges of rivers and ditches along roads and meadows.

Medicinal properties: The queen of the meadow is used as painkiller in joint, muscular, rheumatic and dental pain, but is also effective for headaches, flu-like conditions with fever and body aches. It has a beneficial draining effect as part of a slimming or anti-cellulite diet. It also has cicatrizing, antispasmodic and sudorific properties.

Sage - *Salvia officinalis*

Description, components, used parts

Sage (*Salvia officinalis*) is a sub-shrub that is also called sacred grass. Its stems are of square section, at the lignified base. The leaves are pale green, oblong with a whitish top, persisting in winter thanks to the woolly hair covering that protects them. The flowers on floral stems are blue or pink.

Its name comes from the Latin salvare which means «to save», «to cure». It is one of the sacred plants of the ancients and its medicinal properties have given rise to the saying: **"who has sage in his garden, does not need a doctor"**.

Flowered tops and leaves are dried for therapeutic purposes.

Habitat

Common in Europe, especially in the southern regions, sage is quite rare in the wild. Sage has been cultivated for a very long time.

Medicinal properties: Sage has antiseptic, stimulating, tonic properties. It facilitates digestion and is used in the treatment of diabetes because it decreases blood sugar levels. It is beneficial in case of excessive sweating due to hot flushes during menopause. The herbal tea also has an excellent action on the liver, cramps, night sweats.

St John's wort - *Hypericum Perforatum*

Description, components, used parts
St John's wort (*Hypericum perforatum L.*) is a perennial herb with yellow flowers. These are the flowering tops, picked at the beginning of flowering and dried, which are used in herbal teas.
Habitat
St John's wort is widespread in fields, flowery meadows, by the wayside and in the gardens.

Medicinal properties:
St. John's Wort has antidepressant, digestive, relaxing properties. It is beneficial for panic attacks, attention disorders, mood swings, sleep disorders and menopause.

Wild angelica - *Angelica sylvestris*

Description, components, used parts
Wild angelica Is a large herbaceous plant with a strong stem up to 2-3 m tall. It has white flowers, arranged in parasols. Leaves are alternate, very large, lanceolate. The fruits (= seeds) are creamy yellow or light brown, oval, elongated and flattened. **Garden angelica** (*Angelica archangelica*) is most use

than the wild one - its root and seeds.

Formerly it was called **fever grass** and considered a magical plant. According to legend, it was brought by an angel to a monk revealing its virtues: it protects children, fights the plague, cures the bites of the rabid beasts and chases the devil.

Habitat

Angelica is found in moist grasslands. If you plant it in your garden, it needs light, but also moisture and soil rich in nutrients.

Medicinal properties: Angelica has antispasmodic, tonic, stimulating and carminative properties. It is also a very good anti-stress plant.

Wild chamomile - *Matricaria recutita*

Description, components, used parts

Wild chamomile (*Matricaria recutita*) is a herbaceous plant, used since antiquity. Not to be confused with two other medicinal plants, also called "chamomile": the (*Tanacetum parthenium*) and (*Chamaemelum nobile*).

The leaves are very sharp, almost filiform and the flowers are small, with white petals, recognizing their characteristic odor. Flowering occurs between May and November. The flowers can be used fresh or dried.

Habitat

Wild chamomile is present in Europe, in temperate Asia, in North Africa. In France, it is found in all regions in the wild especially along roads, on waste or cultivated land, saline steppes or on sandy soils, at low altitude.

Medicinal properties: Chamomile is used in digestive disorders and to stimulate appetite. It calms dermatological ailments and eyes. It has antibacterial, cicatrizing, calming and sedative properties. It facilitates digestion and calms digestive cramps, as well as joint pain.

Wild strawberry

Description, components, used parts

Wild strawberries are the fruits of the *Fragaria vesca*. The leaves of the base are trifoliate, toothed. The wild strawberries are reddish or whitish-yellow and have an oblong ovoid shape more or less rounded. They are very fragrant and have a sweet and delicate flavor.

All parts of the plant have a medicinal use. The leaves are rich in tannins, silica and mineral salts, but also vitamin C.

The herbal teas are very fragrant and exquisite taste.

Habitat

Wild strawberries are found in Europe, North America and temperate Asia in the woods, clearings, wood edges, wooded grass paths.

Medicinal properties: The wild strawberries have astringent, diuretic and antirheumatic virtues. Herbal teas are beneficial for gout, kidney stones and urinary diseases. Rich in iron, they are recommended for people with anemia and tuberculosis.

Herbal teas for acne

The acne is a skin condition that occurs in adolescence and is related to sebum hypersecretion. We all experienced the embarrassment caused by the pimples that "flourish" on our face being a teen. Well this problem may continue to appear even later. If you want to prevent or minimize the effects of acne, here are some natural remedies that will do good, for you or your teens :-).

RECIPE 1
Mask with garlic, white clay and honey

Natural masks of garlic juice with honey, have beneficial effects for seborrheic dyes with acne.

Ingredients : 1 garlic cloves, 2 spoonfuls of honey, 1 spoonful of white clay, water

Method : Crush the garlic clove and mix it with a spoonful of white clay and honey. Add a little water if necessary, in order to obtain a thick paste. Tie your hair and apply a thin layer of mixture over the entire face. Let it act for 15 minutes, and rinse with cold water.

RECIPE 2
Dandelion root herbal tea

It is a herbal tea that can fight acne by fighting toxins that unbalance the hormones.

Ingredients : 1 teaspoon dried dandelion root

Method : Boil 1 teaspoon of dried root per large cup of water for 2 minutes. Then let infuse for 10 minutes. Filter before drinking. Sweeten with honey if necessary.

Dose : 2-3 cups / day.

RECIPE 3
Sage tea

Ingredients : 1 tbsp (tablespoon) of dried sage for 100 ml water

Method: Prepare an infusion with 1 tablespoon of dried sage for 100 ml of boiling water and leave about ten minutes. Let it cool a little and apply compresses on the affected parts.

RECIPE 4
Dyeing of greater plantain

Ingredients : 100 g dried leaves of greater plantain, 1 liter alcohol of 70°

Method : Let the leaves macerate in alcohol overnight. Filter and apply compresses to the face in areas affected by acne. This dye is also effective in mouth washes for gingivitis, canker sores, dental pain and other infections.

Dose : 2 to 3 compresses or gargles / day

Herbal teas for allergies

Allergy is a phenomenon of pathological exaggeration of the immune response, in particular the inflammatory reaction. It is an ailment more and more widespread.

RECIPE 5
Lamb's-ear herbal tea

This herbal tea can be used in the treatment of hay fever.

Ingredients : 1 tablespoon per cup of dried plant

Method : Make an infusion for about ten minutes. Filter.

Pour a dozen drops into each nostril, 4 times a day.

RECIPE 6
Nettle herbal tea

Ingredients : 2 tablespoons fresh or dried nettles

Method : Infuse 2 tablespoons of nettle leaves fresh or dried for one liter of boiling water and leave about ten minutes. Filter before drinking.

Dose : 2 cups / day.

Anemia is an abnormality of the hemogram characterized by a decrease in hemoglobin.

Here are some herbal teas that can be beneficial if you suffer from anemia.

RECIPE 7
Herbal tea of wild strawberries and oranges

Ingredients : 1-2 teaspoon of dried wild strawberries, 1 orange

Method : Boil 1 teaspoon of dried plants with the zest of an orange in a liter of water. Filter before drinking and add orange juice.

Dose : 3 cups / day.

RECIPE 8
Herbal tea of nettle with lemon

Ingredients : 1 tablespoon of dried nettles, 1 lemon

Method : Prepare an infusion for a large cup of boiling water and leave about ten minutes. Filter and add the lemon juice before drinking.

Dose : 2-3 cups / day.

The gall bladder is an organ that is found in the abdomen against the liver. The principal function of the vesicle is the storage of the bile in view of its restitution during digestion. Several conditions may affect this organ.

Here are some herbal teas that can be beneficial for gall bladder ailments.

RECIPE 9
Lemon ginger herbal tea

Ginger is beneficial for gallbladder insufficiency.

Ingredients : 1 teaspoon of ginger, 1 lemon

Method : Infuse for a few minutes a teaspoon of fresh or dried ginger for a cup of water. Filter before drinking and add lemon juice.

Dose : 1 cup / day..

RECIPE 10
Lemon and laurel tea

Ingredients : 10 g laurel leaves; 1 lemon

Method : In infusion, let the laurel leaves macerate in 1 liter of water. Filter before drinking and add the lemon juice. If it is too sour or bitter, add some honey.

Dose : 2 - 3 cups / day

RECIPE 11
Marigold herbal tea

Ingredients : 2 teaspoons of dried marigold flowers

Method : Infuse for 5 minutes two teaspoons of

dried flowers for a cup of boiling water. Filter before drinking..
Dose : 2 - 3 cups / day

Cellulite is a small "discomfort" that women know very well and that corresponds to an appearance of orange peel spontaneously or as a result of the pinching of the skin. It is present mainly in the thighs, buttocks and hips.

Here is a herbal tea that can be beneficial for decreasing cellulite.

RECIPE 12
Meadowsweet herbal tea

Ingredients : 1 teaspoon of dried meadowsweet

Method : Infuse for 10-15 minutes a dried plant teaspoon per cup of water. Filter and sweeten with honey before drinking.
Dose : 3 cups / day.

Many of us have problems with blood circulation. Heat is an aggravating factor and our legs suffer during summer ... Because of the stagnation of the blood in the lower part of the body, the heat causes a dilation of the veins, which can weaken their wall compromising in the long run their elasticity.
Here are some herbal teas that can be beneficial by thinning the blood and strengthening the veins.

RECIPE 13
Dog-rose tea

Ingredients : 3 dried fruits per cup

Method : Make a decoction for 2 minutes, then let infuse 10 minutes. Filter before drinking.
Dose : 2 à 3 cups / day.

RECIPE 14
Lime tea with honey

Ingredients : 4 4 lime bracts, honey

Method : Infuse 4 dried bracts for 1 cup of boiling water for 5 minutes. Filter and sweeten with lime honey before drinking.
Dose : 2 to 3 cups / day.

Herbal teas for lowering cholesterol

Here are some herbal teas that can be beneficial to fight bad cholesterol.

RECIPE 15
Ginger tea

Ingredients : 1 teaspoon of ginger

Method : Let infuse for a few minutes a teaspoon of fresh or dried ginger for a cup of water. Filter before drinking.
Dose : 1 cup / day.

RECIPE 16
Oregano tea

Ingredients : 1 teaspoon oregano dried leaves and flowers

Method : Add boiling water to 1 teaspoon of dried oregano leaves and flowers and let infuse for about 10 minutes. Filter before drinking.

Dose : 2-3 cups / day

RECIPE 17
Greater plantain tea

Ingredients : 1 or 2 teaspoons of dried leaves of greater plantain

Method : Add 250 ml of boiling water to 1 to 2 teaspoons of dried leaves and let infuse for about ten minutes. Filter before drinking..

Dose : 3 to 4 cups / day

Herbal teas for conjunctivitis

Conjunctivitis is an inflammation of the mucous membranes lining the eyelids, usually benign.

It is important to consult a doctor who will prescribe antibiotic eye drops if you have a bacterial infection.

Here are some herbal teas that can be beneficial to your eyes.

RECIPE 18
Cornflower and chamomile herbal tea

Ingredients : 1/2 teaspoon of cornflowers and 1/2 teaspoon of chamomile

Method : Make a decoction by bringing to a boil for a few minutes the plants plunged in the water. Let it cool a little and apply compresses on the affected eyes.

RECIPE 19
Lamb's-ear herbal tea

Ingredients : 1 tablespoon dried Lamb's-ear per cup

Method : Make an infusion for about ten minutes. Filter. Let it cool a little and make compresses on the affected eyes.

Herbal teas for heart disease

As you know, the heart is our vital organ and therefore the one we must take the most care of.

Here are some herbal teas that can be beneficial to protect and strengthen your heart.

RECIPE 20
Lemon and flax tea

Ingredients : 2 tablespoon of flax, water, 1 lemon

Method : Macerate overnight 2 tablespoons of seeds to 500 ml of water. In the morning, boil for 5 minutes. Filter before drinking and add lemon juice.

Dose : 1 cup / day

RECIPE 21
Oregano tea

Ingredients : 1 teaspoon of dried leaves and flowers of

oregano

Method : Add boiling water to 1 teaspoon of dried oregano leaves and flowers and let infuse for about 10 minutes. Filter before drinking.

Dose : 2-3 cups / day

RECIPE 22
Honey and greater plantain Syrup

A cure with greater plantain syrup strengthens the heart, but also lungs and detoxifies blood and liver.

Ingredients : 1 to 2 handful of fresh leaves of greater plantain, honey

Method : Wash the leaves and cut them finely. Put them in a saucepan and add a liter of water and 3-4 tablespoons of honey. Continue to blend slowly until the liquid thickens. Put the syrup in closed bottles in the fridge.

Dose : 1 teaspoon before each meal for 2-3 weeks

Herbal teas to fight against constipation

Intestinal transit can be a cause not only of stress, but can generate many other problems.

Here are some herbal teas that can fight constipation.

RECIPE 23
Flax tea

Ingredients : 2 tablespoon of flax, water

Method : Macerate overnight 2 tablespoons of seeds for 500 ml of water. In the morning, boil for 3 minutes. Filter before drinking.

Dose : 1 cup before meal

RECIPE 24
Elderberry herbal tea

Ingredients : 1 teaspoon of dried elderberry

Method : Make an infusion for about ten minutes with a teaspoon of elderberries per cup of boiling water. Filter before drinking and sweeten with honey if necessary.
Dose : 3 cups / day

RECIPE 25
Greater plantain powder herbal tea

Ingredients : 1 to 2 teaspoons of dried greater plantain seeds' powder

Method : Add 1 teaspoon of greater plantain seed powder to a cup of boiling water and leave to infuse for about 10 minutes. Filter before drinking.
Dose : 3 to 4 cups / day

Herbal teas to prevent diabetes

Diabetes refers to a syndrome characterized by increased urine production, necessarily accompanied by excessive thirst. Diabetes mellitus is the most common and is linked to an abnormal synthesis of insulin.

Here are some herbal teas that can prevent the onset of this syndrome.

RECIPE 26
Nettle tea

Ingredients : 1 tablespoon of dried nettles

Method : Prepare an infusion for one liter of boiling

water and let infuse for 5-10 minutes. Filter before drinking. As nettle exerts an influence on the pancreas, nettle tea lowers the blood sugar level.

Dose : 2 cups / day.

RECIPE 27
Sage tea

Ingredients : 1 teaspoon of dried sage per cup

Method : Prepare an infusion with 1 teaspoon of dried sage per cup of boiling water and leave about ten minutes. Filter before drinking.

Dose : 2-3 cups / day.

Herbal teas to combat diarrhea

We were all one day or another victim of diarrhea. Here are some herbal teas that can fight it.

RECIPE 28
Mint tea

The best herbal tea to combat diarrhea and abdominal colic remain the mint one. I have always used this herbal tea for all my family and it has always worked very well! Even tea bags sold in supermarkets work well, even if the dried plant gives results faster.

Ingredients : 1 teaspoon of fresh or dried mint

Method : Prepare an infusion of a mint teaspoon for a large cup of boiling water. Leave 5 minutes and filter before drinking.

Dose : 2-3 cups / day.

RECIPE 29
Basil herbal tea

Ingredients : 1 teaspoon of basil

Method : Prepare an infusion for a large cup of boiling water. Let it act for 10 minutes. Filter before drinking.
Dose : 2 to 3 cups / day.

RECIPE 30
Dog-rose tea

Ingredients : 40g powdered fruit per liter.

Method : Put 40 g of fruit powder per liter of boiling water and let infuse for 15 minutes. Filter before drinking.
Dose : 2 to 3 cups / day.

Herbal teas to detoxify the liver

The liver has a very important role in our body.
Here are some herbal teas that can be beneficial to the liver.

RECIPE 31
Herbal root tea of wild chicory and dandelion

Ingredients : 1 tablespoon of wild chicory roots and 1 tablespoon of dandelion roots

Method : Boil for 5 minutes a tablespoon of plants per cup of water, then let infuse for 10 minutes. Filter before drinking. Attention, the taste is not amazing...
Dose : 1 cup in the morning and 1 in the evening.

RECIPE 32
Lovage herbal tea with lemon

Ingredients : 1 tablespoon lovage and 1 lemon

Method : Prepare an infusion for 10 minutes, 1 tablespoon of lovage for 250 ml of water. Filter and add the lemon juice before drinking.

Dose : 2 to 3 cups / day.

RECIPE 33
Dandelion and nettles tea

Ingredients : 1 handful of fresh dandelion leaves and another of nettles

Method : Wash the leaves well. Let them infuse by pouring 500 ml of boiling water on them and leave 5 minutes. Filter before drinking. Sweeten with honey if necessary.

Dose : 2-3 cups / day.

RECIPE 34
Horsetail tea

Ingredients : 2 tablespoons of dried horsetail

Method : Let macerate overnight 2 tablespoons of plants per half liter of water. In the morning warm up and filter before drinking..

Dose : 1/2 liter per day in several doses.

RECIPE 35
Honey marigold herbal tea

Ingredients : 2 teaspoons of dried marigold flowers, 1 teaspoon of honey

Method : Let infuse for 5 minutes two teaspoons of dried flowers for a cup of boiling water. Filter and sweeten with honey before drinking.

Dose : 2 - 3 cups / day

Herbal teas for high blood pressure

Hypertension is a cardiovascular disease characterized by high blood pressure.

Here are some herbal teas that can be beneficial for hypertension by lowering it naturally or by preventing it.

RECIPE 36
Herbal tea of garlic and orange

Ingredients : 1 garlic clove, 1-2 teaspoon of dried orange skins

Method : For a few minutes, infuse one or two teaspoons of dried orange peel with a clove of peeled garlic and cut into pieces.

Filter before drinking.

RECIPE 37
Greater plantain tea

Ingredients : 1 teaspoon of dried seeds of greater plantain

Method : Add 250 ml of boiling water to 1 teaspoon of dried seeds and let infuse for about 10 minutes. Filter before drinking.

Dose : 3 cups / day

RECIPE 38
Lemon celery tea

Ingredients : 2 celery stalks with leaves, juice and zest of a lemon, 1 liter of water

Method : Wash the celery and lemon thoroughly. Put the water to boil and when it boils, add the cut celery and the lemon peel. Let another 5 to 10 minutes at low heat. Let rest for about 10 minutes and add the lemon juice.

Dose : 1 to 2 cups / day

RECIPE 39
Hawthorn fruit tea

Ingredients : 1 teaspoon of dried fruit of hawthorn

Method : Make a decoction by boiling 5 minutes one teaspoon per cup. Filter before drinking.

Herbal teas to fight indigestion

An indigestion is the rejection by the digestive system of a recent meal. Here are some herbal teas that can prevent indigestion and be beneficial for digestion.

RECIPE 40
Fresh lemon balm herbal tea

Ingredients : 1 or 2 branches with leaves of fresh lemon balm

Method : Dive into a liter of water 2 branches of lemon balm and boil. Then let infuse 10-15 minutes. Filter and let cool before drinking. This herbal tea is even better fresh.

Dose : 1/2 cups per day

RECIPE 41
St. John's wort tea with honey

Attention this herbal tea has a slightly bitter taste.
Ingredients : 1 teaspoon of St. John's wort, 1 teaspoon of honey

Method : In infusion, leave 10 minutes a teaspoon of dried St. John's wort for a large cup of water. Filter before drinking. Add acacia honey, which is an excellent intestinal regulator.
Dose : 2 to 3 cups / day

RECIPE 42
Sage and chamomile tea

Ingredients : 1 teaspoon of dried sage and one of chamomile per cup

Method : Prepare an infusion with 1 teaspoon of dried sage and one of chamomile per cup of boiling water and leave about 10 minutes. Filter before drinking.
Dose : 2-3 cups / day.

Herbal teas for insomnia

Insomnia is represented by sleep disorders. Here are some herbal teas that can be beneficial against insomnia.

RECIPE 43
Motherwort tea

Ingredients : 2 teaspoon of dried plants

Method : Prepare an infusion of 2 teaspoons of dried plants for a cup of boiling water. Filter before drinking.
Dose : 2-3 cups / day.

RECIPE 44
Orange and chamomile herbal tea

Ingredients : 1 teaspoon chamomile, 1 orange

Method : Prepare an infusion for 10 minutes, at a rate of 1 teaspoon per cup. You can also add orange zest (after having washed it well) to perfume your tea. Filter before drinking. Add the orange juice.

Dose : 2 to 3 cups / day.

RECIPE 45
Lavender tea

The taste of lavender tea is very fragrant and pleasant, but be careful if you are allergic! (Better to avoid drinking it in this case)

Ingredients : 1,5 teaspoon of dried flowers per cup

Method : Prepare an infusion for 5 to 10 minutes, one to two teaspoons of lavender per cup. Filter before drinking.

Dose : 1 cup before sleeping

RECIPE 46
Poppy tea

Ingredients : 1 tablespoon of dried petals per cup

Method : Prepare an infusion for 10 minutes, one tablespoon per cup. Filter before drinking.

Dose : 2 à 3 cups / day.

RECIPE 47
Lime tea with honey

Ingredients : 4 lime bracts, honey

Method : Let infuse 4 dried bracts for 1 cup of boiling water for 5 minutes. Filter and sweeten with lime honey if possible before drinking.
Dose : 2 to 3 cups / day.

Herbal teas to strengthen immune defenses

Immunity is the state of equilibrium which is characterized by adequate biological defenses to combat infection, disease, or other biological invasion undesirable to the organism.

Here are some herbal teas that can be beneficial for enhancing immunity.

RECIPE 48
Herbal tea of cowberry, honey and orange

Ingredients : 1 teaspoon of dried berries or leaves of cowberry, 1 teaspoon dried orange peel, 1 tablespoon honey

Method : Let infuse for a few minutes a teaspoon of dried berries or cowberry leaves with a teaspoon of dried orange skins. Filter and sweeten with honey.

RECIPE 49
Nettle herbal tea with honey

Ingredients : 1 tablespoon dried nettles, 1 teaspoon honey

Method : Prepare an infusion for a large cup of boiling water and leave about ten minutes. Filter and sweeten

with fir honey preferably before drinking. Fir honey is rich in trace elements such as phosphorus, potassium, calcium, sulfur, magnesium, zinc, boron, iron and copper.
Dose : 2-3 cups / day.

RECIPE 50
Narrow-leaved purple coneflower herbal tea

Ingredients : 1/2 teaspoon per cup

Method : Make a decoction for 2 minutes, then let infuse during 5 minutes.
Filter before drinking.
Dose : 2 cups / day.

RECIPE 51
Orange and marigold tea

Ingredients : 2 teaspoons of dried marigold flowers, 1 orange, few drops essence of orange blossom

Method : Infuse for 5 minutes two teaspoons of dried flowers for a cup of boiling water. Filter before drinking. Add the juice of an orange and a few drops of orange blossom essence.
Dose : 2 - 3 cups / day

Herbal teas to combat fatigue

Fatigue is a fairly common complaint in our society today. It may be physiological or psychological, but it diminishes us as much...

So here are some herbal teas that can be beneficial to fight fatigue and that will give you back tone :-).

RECIPE 52
Hawthorn herbal tea

Ingredients : 1-2 teaspoon of dried flowers and / or fruit of hawthorn

Method : Prepare an infusion for a large cup of boiling water. Filter before drinking..

Dose : 2 to 3 cups / day.

RECIPE 53
Blackcurrant tea

Ingredients : 1 tablespoon of dried blackcurrant leaves and fruits

Method : Prepare an infusion based on a tablespoonful of blackcurrant for a large cup of boiling water and leave for about ten minutes. Filter before drinking.

Dose : 2 to 3 cups / day.

RECIPE 54
Dog-rose berries tea

Ingredients : 1-2 dried fruits per cup.

Method : Make an infusion for about ten minutes

with one or two fruits per cup of boiling water. Filter before drinking and sweeten with honey if necessary.

Dose : 3 cups / day.

Excess weight is one of the problems of our century.

Here are some herbal teas that can fight against obesity and be beneficial in slimming cures.

RECIPE 55
Lemon celery tea

Ingredients : 3 celery stalks with leaves, lemon juice, 1 liter of water

Method : Thoroughly wash the celery stalks. Put the water to boil and when it does, put the celery cut. Leave another 5 to 10 minutes at low heat. Leave to rest for about 10 minutes and add the lemon juice.

Dose : 1 to 3 cups / day before meals.

RECIPE 56
Lemon blackcurrant tea

Ingredients : 1 tablespoon of blackcurrant, 1 lemon

Method : Prepare an infusion based on a tablespoon of blackcurrant for a large cup of boiling water and leave for about ten minutes. Filter and add the lemon juice before drinking.

Dose : 3 cups / day.

RECIPE 57
Wild chicory tea

Ingredients : 1 tablespoon of dried chicory per cup

Method : Make an infusion for 2 minutes at a rate of one tablespoon per cup of water. Filter before drinking..
Dose : 2-3 cups / day.

RECIPE 58
Lovage herbal tea with lemon

Ingredients : 1 tablespoon of lovage and 1 lemon

Method : Prepare an infusion for 10 minutes, 1 tablespoon of lovage for 250 ml of water. Filter and add the lemon juice before drinking.
Dose : 2-3 cups / day.

Herbal teas for migraine

Migraine is a headache that can even generate nausea and can be quite disabling.
Here are some herbal teas that can be beneficial against migraine.

RECIPE 59
Ginger tea

This is the most powerful remedy we have found so far (Olivier often has migraines) and it quickly relieves pain (within 15-30 minutes).
Ingredients : 1 teaspoon of chamomile, 1 lemon, 1 tablespoon of honey

Method : Peel a piece of fresh ginger and prepare a decoction for 10 minutes, then let infuse for another 10 minutes. In order to accelerate the beneficial effect, chew the ginger slices (but be careful, the taste is rather strong and not really pleasant)!

Dose : the effect is quite fast, but if the migraine goes on, you may drink 3 cups / day.

RECIPE 60
Lovage tea

Ingredients : 1 tablespoon of lovage

Method : Prepare an infusion for 10 minutes, at the rate of 1 tablespoon for 250 ml of water. Filter before drinking.

Dose: 1 to 3 cups / day.

RECIPE 61
Breckland thyme herbal tea with honey

Ingredients : 1 teaspoon of dried Breckland thyme, 1 teaspoon of honey

Method : Infuse a teaspoon of dried Breckland thyme in a cup of water for about ten minutes. Filter before drinking and add thyme honey if possible.

Dose : 2-3 cups / day.

Herbal teas for menopause

Menopause corresponds to a hormonal fall at the end of the reproductive period of the woman. It appears from the age of forty and is manifested by hot flushes, night sweats, irregular periods, bloating sensations, mood swings, irritability, breast tensions.

Here are some herbal teas that can be beneficial for menopause.

RECIPE 62
Motherwort and sage tea

Ingredients : 1 teaspoon of dried plants of Motherwort and one of sage

Method : Prepare an infusion of 2 teaspoons of dried plants for a cup of boiling water. Filter before drinking.
Dose : 2-3 cups / day.

RECIPE 63
St. John's wort tea with honey

Ingredients : 1 teaspoon of St. John's wort, 1 teaspoon of honey

Method : In infusion, let 10 minutes a teaspoon of dried St. John's wort in a large cup of water. Filter and sweeten with honey before drinking.
Dose : 2 to 3 cups / day

Osteoporosis is characterized by the excessive fragility of the skeleton, due to a decrease in bone mass. It affects women more than men.

Here are some herbal teas that can be beneficial against osteoporosis and that tend to strengthen your bones.

RECIPE 64
Nettle herbal tea with orange

Ingredients : 2 tablespoons of nettles, 1 orange

Method : Infuse 2 tablespoons of nettle leaves - fresh or dried - with one tablespoon of dried orange skins in one liter of boiling water and leave for about ten minutes. Filter and add orange juice before drinking.

Dose : 2-3 cups / day.

RECIPE 65
Horsetail tea

Ingredients : 1 teaspoon dried horsetail

Method : Infuse for 10-15 minutes a dried plant teaspoon per cup of water. Filter and sweeten with honey before drinking.

Dose : 1-2 cups / day.

Herbal teas for respiratory diseases

A respiratory disease affects the respiratory system or causes breathing problems.

Here are some herbal teas that can be beneficial for respiratory ailments and that will strengthen your lungs.

RECIPE 66
Herbal tea of garlic, thyme and honey

Ingredients : 1 teaspoon of thyme, 1 garlic clove, 1 teaspoon honey

Method : Infuse for a few minutes a teaspoon of thyme with a clove of peeled garlic and cut into pieces.

Filter and sweeten with honey if needed.

Dose : 2 cups / day.

RECIPE 67
Inhalation with basil

For respiratory infections such as rhinitis or during an influenza, basil inhalations are effective.

Ingredients : 1 teaspoon basil

Method : Boil 1 teaspoon of basil in a large cup of water.

Make an inhalation in the morning and in the evening.

RECIPE 68
Borage tea

Ingredients : 2 teaspoons of borage

Method : Prepare an infusion for 10 minutes, at the

rate of 2 teaspoons per cup. Filter before drinking.
Dose : 2 to 3 cups / day.

RECIPE 69
Lavender tea with honey

The taste of lavender tea is very fragrant and pleasant, but be careful if you are allergic! (Better to avoid drinking in this case) This herbal tea is indicated for asthmatics.

Ingredients : 1,5 teaspoons of dried flowers per cup, 1 teaspoon of honey

Method : Prepare an infusion for 10 minutes, one to two teaspoons per cup. Filter and sweeten with honey before drinking.

Dose : 2 to 3 cups / day.

RECIPE 70
Oregano tea with honey

Ingredients : 1 teaspoon of dried oregano, 1 teaspoon of honey

Method : Add boiling water to 1 teaspoon of dried oregano leaves and flowers and let infuse for about 10 minutes. Filter and sweeten with a spoon of honey, preferably eucalyptus.

Dose : 2-3 cups / day

Herbal teas for rheumatism

Rheumatism affects joints and connective tissue. Osteoarthritis is a disease that affects the joints by causing pain and discomfort.

Here are some herbal teas that can be beneficial against rheumatism, osteoarthritis, and that strengthen your joints.

RECIPE 71
Cornflower tea

The cornflower tea has a delicate and fragrant taste that you will probably enjoy ;-).

Ingredients : 1 teaspoon of cornflower/cup

Method : Prepare an infusion for 3 to 5 minutes. Filter before drinking.

Dose : 2 to 3 cups / day.

RECIPE 72
Celery and orange tea

Ingredients : 2 celery stalks with leaves, 1 orange, 1 liter of water

Method : Thoroughly wash the celery stalks and the orange. Put the water to boil and when it does, add the cut celery and the zest of the orange. Leave another 5 to 10 minutes at low heat. Leave to stand for about 10 minutes and add orange juice.

Dose : 2 to 3 cups / day.

RECIPE 73
Parsley and orange tea

Ingredients : 1 small parsley root and 1 orange

Method : Wash the parsley and orange thoroughly. Make a decoction by bringing to a boil for 5 to 10 minutes the parsley peeled and cut into pieces and the pulp of the orange after extracting the juice. Filter before drinking and add the orange juice.

Dose : 2 to 3 cups / day.

RECIPE 74
Orange and blackcurrant tea

It is a herbal tea with a very aromatic taste and which is likely to please you if you like blackcurrant ;-)...

Ingredients : 1 tablespoon of dried blackcurrant, 1 orange

Method : Prepare an infusion based on a tablespoonful of blackcurrant for a cup of boiling water and the zest of an orange and leave for about ten minutes. Filter before drinking and add the orange juice.

Dose : 3 cups / day.

RECIPE 75
Elderberry herbal tea

Ingredients : 1 teaspoon dried elderberry

Method : Make an infusion of about ten minutes with a teaspoon of elderberries per cup of boiling water. Filter before drinking and sweeten with honey if necessary.

Dose : 3-4 cups / day

Herbal teas to combat stress

You know all what stress is and maybe you experience it more or less regularly...

Here are some herbal teas that can fight stress and be beneficial for relaxation.

RECIPE 76
Motherwort and hawthorn tea

Ingredients : 1 teaspoon of dried plants of Motherwort and 1/2 teaspoon of hawthorn

Method : Prepare an infusion for a large cup of boiling water. Filter before drinking.

Dose : 2 cups / day.

RECIPE 77
Angelica tea

Ingredients : 1 tablespoon angelica's root and / or seeds

Method : Boil for 2 minutes and then let infuse for 5 to 10 minutes a tablespoon of seeds or root per cup. Filter before drinking.

Dose : 1-2 cups / day.

RECIPE 78
St. John's wort tea with orange and honey

Ingredients : 1 teaspoon St. John's wort, 1 orange, 1 teaspoon of honey

Method : In infusion, leave 10 minutes a teaspoon of

dried St. John's wort with the zest of an orange for a large cup of water. Filter before drinking. Add the juice of an orange and sweeten with honey if needed.

Dose : 2 to 3 cups / day

RECIPE 79
Hyssop and orange tea

Ingredients : 1 teaspoon of hyssop, 1 orange

Method : Infuse for a few minutes a hyssop teaspoon and two teaspoons of dried orange skins. Filter before drinking.

Dose : 2-3 cups / day.

RECIPE 80
Laurel tea

Ingredients : 10-15 g of laurel leaves

Method : In infusion, let macerate 10-15 g of bay leaves in 1 liter of water.

Dose : 2 to 3 cups per day, after meals.

RECIPE 81
Melissa herbal tea

Ingredients : 1 tablespoon of lemon balm

Method : In infusion, leave 10-15 minutes a tablespoon of lemon balm for a large cup of water.

Dose : 1 to 2 cups per day.

Herbal teas to soothe cough and throat irritations

Here are some herbal teas that can be beneficial for coughing and irritations of the throat.

RECIPE 82
Honey poppy tea

Ingredients : 1 tablespoon of dried petals per cup, 1 tablespoon of honey

Method : Prepare an infusion for 10 minutes, one tablespoon per cup. Filter and sweeten with honey before drinking.
Dose : 2 to 3 cups / day.

RECIPE 83
Hyssop herbal tea

Ingredients : 1 teaspoon hyssop

Method : Infuse a teaspoon of dried hyssop for a cup of water. Filter before drinking..
Dose : 2-3 cups / day.

RECIPE 84
Breckland thyme herbal tea

Ingredients : 1 teaspoon of dried Breckland thyme

Method : Infuse a teaspoon of dried Breckland thyme for about ten minutes for a cup of water. Filter before drinking.
Dose : 2-3 cups / day.

RECIPE 85
Honey and greater plantain Syrup

A cure with greater plantain syrup strengthens the heart, but also lungs and detoxifies blood and liver

Ingredients : 1 to 2 handful of fresh leaves of greater plantain, honey

Method : Wash the leaves and cut them finely. Put them in a saucepan and add a liter of water and 3-4 tablespoons of honey. Continue to blend slowly until the liquid thickens. Put the syrup in closed bottles in the fridge.

Dose : 1 to 3 teaspoons per day

Herbal teas for urinary tract infections

The urinary disorders can be of very different natures..

RECIPE 86
Cowberry tea

Ingredients : 2 teaspoon fresh or dried cowberry berries or leaves

Method : Infuse two teaspoons of fresh or dried cowberry berries or leaves for a few minutes. Filter before drinking.

Dose : 2 cups / day.

RECIPE 87
Herbal tea of cherry tails

Ingredients : 1 tablespoon of cherry tails per cup

Method : First make a decoction for 3 minutes, then let infuse for 10 minutes. Filter before drinking.

Dose : 2-3 cups / day.

RECIPE 88
Couch grass tea

Ingredients : 1 teaspoon of dried couch grass rhizomes per cup

Method : Make a decoction for 3 minutes, with 1 teaspoon of couch grass. Filter before drinking.
Dose : 2-3 cups / day.

RECIPE 89
Wild Strawberry tea

Ingredients : 2 teaspoons of dried plants

Method : Boil 2 teaspoons of dried plants in a liter of water.
Filter before drinking.
Dose : 2-3 cups / day.

Here are some herbal drinks that not only have healing properties, but also exquisite flavors. Some of these drinks I've known since my childhood since my parents used to replace the non-existent sodas with them in my country at that time ;-) ... I have discovered later other drinks and appreciated them, so I share them with you in this section :-).

RECIPE 90
Socata - elderflower drink

A great refreshing drink that I would warmly recommend!

Ingredients : 10 Elderberry inflorescences, 500 g brown sugar, 2 lemons, 8 g baker's yeast

Method : Wash the elderflowers and put them in a 5 liter jar. Add sugar, sliced lemons. Add water until covered and cover the jar with a cloth. The next day, fill the jar with cold water and mix. Add the yeast, cover the jar and leave in a warm and sunny place for 2 or 3 days. Mix every morning and evening and taste it. When the acidity of the beverage suits you, filter and put it in bottles in the refrigerator. The socata should be better if you drink it very fresh.

RECIPE 91
Liqueur of angelica

For liquor enthusiasts, here is a liqueur with delicate fragrance, which should be drunk after the meal, in small doses, and which can facilitate the digestion.

Ingredients : 150 g fresh angelica stems, 3 cloves, 1 cinnamon stick, 1 vanilla bean and 1 liter of white rum

Method : In a large jar, put the stems, the vanilla bean cut lengthwise, cinnamon and cloves. Pour the rum over it. Let macerate for 10 days mixing every day.

Filter before drinking.

RECIPE 92
Schrubb or orange liqueur

For alcohol amateurs, here is a perfumed liqueur, native from the West Indies, and which I have tasted in Martinique.

Ingredients : 4 oranges, 2 cinnamon sticks, 1 vanilla bean and 1 liter of white rum and 500 g cane sugar

Method : Prepare an orange essence first: wash the oranges and peel the skin without the white part. Let them dry to the sun for two days. Put them in a jar and add the rum and let macerate 4 days.

Remove the orange peels. Boil the cane sugar with 1/2 liter of water, cinnamon, vanilla until the juice thickens. Mix as much syrup as rum and add 10 cl of orange essence, put it in bottles.

Drink with moderation!

HOW TO GET THE EBOOK FOR FREE

Did you appreciate this guide? Would you like to have an electronic version of it, for free? You could then enjoy it on your smartphone or tablet, and more easily identify the plants thanks to the colored photos, always at your fingertips and friendlier to the environment!

It is easy: just write a review on the platform you bought the paper book and send me an email with a proof of your review and I will send you the epub file right away, into your inbox! Send me an email at: cristina.rebiere@gmail.com

Hoping to read from you soon ☺

Cristina

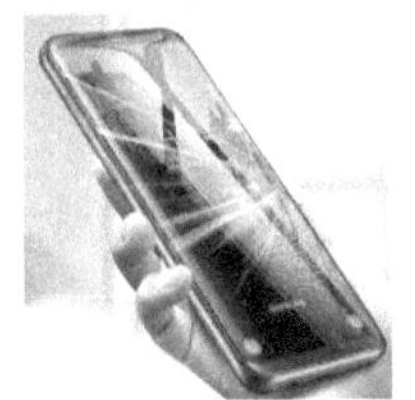

Credits

Thank you to all the kind souls who offer online tools and free resources to use for those who always want to learn and improve!

Authors

Cristina and Olivier Rebière met at the age of 17 in Romania shortly after the fall of the Berlin Wall and the Romanian Revolution of December 1989. After two years of correspondence and several meetings, Cristina was able to get a scholarship to study in France, and she became Olivier's wife in 1993. Since then, these two "adventurers of life" have had a journey full of twists and turns, during which they fell in love with travel, entrepreneurship, and writing. Their books are useful, practical, and will fill you with energy and creativity.

Discover all of Cristina & Olivier's collections on their website http://www.OlivierRebiere.com